Taurus

A collection of cosmic poetry

Denise Grace

ISBN: 979-8-3976-2192-2

DEDICATION

To my dear Taurus friend,

whose unwavering determination and unwavering hearts inspire us to embrace the beauty of stability, this book is dedicated to you.

May your enduring spirit guide you on the path of love, where your loyalty becomes the foundation of cherished relationships. May you find comfort in the depth of your affections and may your commitment shine like a guiding star. In your presence, we learn the power of steadfastness, the art of indulgence, and the beauty of sensual connection. This dedication is a tribute to your enduring love and a reminder of the profound impact you have on those around you.

May this book ignite your passion, nourish your soul, and celebrate the unique magic that lies within you.

CONTENTS

Dear Reader,

As you immerse yourself in the enchanting universe of this poetry collection, I invite you to embrace the diverse world of the zodiac sign Taurus.

Yet, remember that the sun sign alone is just one facet of the complex constellation that is your birth chart. Your celestial identity is a symphony of various planetary influences, weaving a unique melody that resonates within you.

Not every poem may perfectly mirror your own experiences or fully capture the intricate layers that define you. And that is more than okay – it is beautiful. Embrace the delightful diversity within yourself and cherish the individual influences that shape your cosmic dance.

So let these poems ignite your imagination, inspire reflection, and celebrate the vibrant mosaic of your unique astrological identity. May you find resonance, amusement, and the sheer delight of discovering the vastness within you.

With cosmic wonders and infinite possibilities,
Denise

INTRODUCTION

Dear Taurus,

I wanted to take a moment to express my appreciation for all that you are. Your unwavering determination and unyielding spirit inspire awe and admiration in those fortunate enough to witness your journey.

Your steadfastness is a testament to the strength that resides within you. Like a mighty mountain standing tall against the winds of change, you remain grounded and resolute in the face of challenges. Your unwavering commitment to your goals and principles is a beacon of inspiration for us all.

Your practicality is unmatched, bringing stability and order to even the most chaotic of situations. With your feet planted firmly on the ground, you navigate life's twists and turns with grace and precision. Your ability to find beauty in simplicity is a gift that brings joy to those around you.

Your loyalty is a force to be reckoned with, a flame that burns brightly in the hearts of those fortunate enough to be in you life. Your unwavering support and steadfast presence make you a true pillar of strength, offering comfort and security in times of need.

May your steady spirit continue to guide you towards the fulfillment of your dreams. You are a true testament to the beauty and strength that resides within the Taurus' soul.

Sincerely,
Denise

Taurus is the second astrological sign in the zodiac, symbolized by the Bull. People born between April 20 and May 20 fall under this earth sign. Taurus is ruled by Venus, the planet of love and beauty, and is known for its practicality, dependability, and sensuality.

Taurus is a fixed sign and the embodiment of stability and determination. Their fixed nature makes them resolute in their pursuits, holding steadfast to their goals, and providing a solid foundation.

Taurus individuals are often characterized by their grounded nature and strong work ethic. They have a practical approach to life and are very reliable and committed. Taurus individuals value stability and security, and they are willing to put in the necessary effort to achieve their goals.

Taurus is also associated with a love for the finer things in life. They have a refined taste and appreciate beauty, whether it's in art, music, or fashion. Their sensual nature is expressed in their love for indulgent experiences and their ability to savor the pleasures of life.

While Taurus individuals are generally patient and easygoing, they can also be quite stubborn. Once they set their mind on something, it can be challenging to change their perspective. However, this determination and perseverance also makes them resilient and reliable in pursuing their ambitions.

PERSONALITY

In the realm of the bull, there lies a sign,
a Taurus, steadfast, strong, and divine.
Their ruling planet, Venus, guides their way,
a love of beauty, luxury, and display.

With a spirit unyielding, they stand their ground,
their loyalty, steadfast, strong and profound.
Their sensuality, an earthly delight,
a Taurus' touch, a warm and loving light.

With a heart that's open and a mind that's true,
a Taurus friendship, a treasure to pursue.
Their determination, like a mountain's might,
a Taurus' resolve, an unwavering sight.

In the depths of their being, a passion burns,
a Taurus love, an intense desire yearns.
Their connection to the earth, a bond unbroken,
a Taurus' spirit, a force to be awoken.

So let us celebrate this sign so rare,
a Taurus' strength, a gift beyond compare.
Their ruling planet, Venus, shines so bright,
a Taurus' beauty, a wondrous sight.

Like a rock in a river,
a dependable force
that can withstand the flow
of life's challenges.

The ultimate foodie of the zodiac, it's true,
they'll never pass up a chance,
to indulge in a decadent meal or dessert,
indulgence they pursue.

The best in you,
the unwavering determination,
the sensual charm,
the lacey bra,
the grounded stability,
the comforting song on replay,
the loyal protector,
the artistic soul.

Like unyielding mountains,
once their resolve takes hold,
no force can sway their path,
their commitment bold.

Taurus

My heart beats in tune with stability's grace,
Seeking harmony in a world's ever-changing chase.

Radiating warmth,
grounding presence.

A resolute character,
unyielding in its stance.
A spirited soul,
steadfast in its dance.

Reveling in luxury's embrace,
they delight,
in life's finer things,
a taste exquisite and bright,
yet, with a keen eye,
their pennies they hold tight.

A steadfast soul
that embraces stability
and thrives in the comfort
of a grounded existence.

Patient souls,
flowing with tranquility.

The rose bouquet,
the patient eyes,
the loving hug,
the bubble bath,
the sensual touch,
the sound of your favorite song,
with the rainbow just for you.

– the epitome of charm

Practicality is their armor,
navigating life's complexities
with a grounded approach
and a keen eye for practical solutions.

I've always been a realist,
grounded firmly in reality,
where dreams were attainable plans.
I ascend only as high as the counter,
where the fall won't be lethal.

A true foodie sees the world
through the lens of flavors,
savoring every bite
as delicious adventures.

Taurus' mantra is:
"I'll stop being stubborn when I'm convinced I'm wrong...
so basically never."

I don't sugarcoat my words;
I serve them straight up,
with a side of raw honesty.

Sensual beings,
embracing the art of indulgence.

I sway between diligence and leisure's thrall,
for what sparks my heart, I give my all,
but if it lacks allure, I tend to sprawl,
in a state of leisure, heedless of the call.

Anger,
a mirror to their passionate core,
in their determined spirit,
they endure,
they won't abide being treated unfairly,
that's for sure.

Taurus prefers the steady rhythm of the familiar,
where stability reigns and change tiptoes cautiously.

I tread the path of labor with devotion,
then with earned indulgence,
my spirit finds its ocean of serenity.

I am Taurus.
I am the endearing, stubborn child you can't help but adore.
I am your cherished comfort meal, a taste of solace in every bite. I embody the inner child that longs to have its way, and my charm disarms any hint of anger.
I am the unwavering loyalty, a steadfast presence in your life.
I am the scent of fresh soil and blooming roses, a harmonious blend of groundedness and sensuality.
I am the sound of birds chirping in the morning and the symphony orchestra, reflecting your deep appreciation for beauty and sensory pleasures.
I am the everlasting picnic in the park, where time stands still, and joy reigns supreme. The embodiment of patience and determination, I see every endeavor through.
I am the warm embrace that envelops you on a chilly night, offering solace and security.
I am the curator of serenity, creating an oasis of tranquility in a fast-paced world.
I am Taurus, a feast of soothing senses, a banquet for the soul.

Taurus

Patient observers,
they carefully weigh their options,
considering every detail
before making decisions
of great significance.

Confidence as my crown,
a steadfast belief in their abilities renowned,
a resolute sense of self, their strength unbound.

Harmonious blend
of grace and power.

Denise Grace

The magpie of the zodiac,
they adore shiny things,
hording them eagerly,
as if bound by golden wings.

When they choose not to engage,
masters of the art of laziness, they stage,
procrastination their ever-faithful aide.

Goddess of love, oh Venus divine,
in your presence, hearts align.
With grace and beauty, you enchant,
spreading love's magic, tender and grand.

Your radiance shines, a celestial light,
guiding souls through passion's flight.
Through art and music, you inspire,
igniting desires, setting hearts on fire.

Taurus, a fixed earth sign, stands as the unwavering cornerstone of the zodiac. Their stability is matched only by their appreciation for life's sensory pleasures.
Like the earth awakening in spring, Taurus embodies steadfast determination, sensuality, and an unshakable commitment to their path.

Connoisseurs of beauty,
they celebrate life's aesthetics.

Deeply connected to the material world,
they appreciate the finer things in life,
finding solace in the tangible expressions of beauty.

Denise Grace

The patience of a saint,
the perseverance of a marathon runner,
the stubbornness of a mule.

What you see is what you get with them,
no filter in expressing thoughts and opinions,
it's a gem.

To toil and savor,
my efforts returned,
in life's garden,
dreams are earned.

The earthly divine,
sensuous and sublime,
rooted in reality,
yet soaring beyond time.

Reliably and without fuss,
but only with no rush,
or they'll dig in their heels
like a stubborn bull.

Behind a calm demeanor,
sensitivity like a wellspring of emotions,
flowing with both strength and vulnerability.

Their concept of spontaneity,
on a Friday night,
involves rearranging sock drawers,
with sheer delight,
living life on the edge,
in their own unique light.

Practical minds,
finding order in the chaos.

In sensuous delight,
I've known,
cooking,
savoring,
dessert,
on my own.

A flower field in one fleeting moment,
then the Earth cracks open,
devouring all within its grasp in the next.

You are like honey,
a blend of softness and strength,
unwaveringly sticking to your principles,
at times fruity, sometimes earthy,
occasionally bearing a hint of bitterness,
yet always, undeniably honey.

What I love:

Cozy movie nights.
Comfort foods.
Exploring new recipes.
Establishing rituals with loved ones.
Embracing commitment and loyalty.
Nurturing shopping indulgences.
Enjoying leisurely mornings.
Engaging in artistic projects.
Striving to have things my way.
Picnicking amid blooming flowers and lush trees.
Cherishing quality time and physical touch.

Guardian of tradition,
past and present intertwine,
embracing history's wisdom,
a legacy so fine.

There's comfort in the familiar,
I prefer the steady rhythm of stability
over the unpredictable dance of change.

Not shy, but reserved, I stand my ground,
a thinker and observer, in thoughts I'm bound.
In small details, unnoticed by the rest,
I find the beauty, the moments that are best.

In quiet contemplation, my mind takes flight,
unveiling the world's secrets, its hidden light.
I'm the one who listens, who carefully sees,
the beauty in nuances, like a gentle breeze.

Calm and collected on the outside,
but inside,
a volcano of emotions
waiting to erupt.

Beauty is indeed everywhere,
waiting for those who look closely.
It can be found in every hour of every day,
the gentle kiss at the train station,
the girl applying lipstick in a car's window,
the little kid jumping with excitement
at the sight of a big car,
two unfamiliar dogs forming a bond,
the cashier's welcoming smile.

Taurus

Divine soul,
cherry blossom eyes,
breathing in the
beauty of the moment,
dazzling smile,
strawberries
with whipped cream,
gallery openings,
sensual dancing,
soft sing-along,
warming aura.

With unwavering values,
they shine so bright,
Taurus,
the beacon of honesty and right.
their integrity unwavering,
their morals strong,
in their presence,
we know where we belong.

Patience as their virtue,
they navigate with composure.

An umbrella on a sun-kissed day,
a tissue just in case,
a pad, even after I finished my period,
with no time to waste,
an emotional support water bottle,
an extra phone charger, too,
expecting the unexpected,
being organized, in all I pursue.

A compromise,
like a knife in my own back,
I can't betray myself like that.

I've never discovered a middle ground in anything,
be it work, a passion, friendships,
or you.
My way has always been to care intensely,
as if my life hinges on it,
or not to care at all.

Their beliefs held
with an iron grasp so tight,
only divine intervention
could alter their resolute flight.

Bottled-up emotions,
in a paint-filled vessel,
I silently choke,
now, on canvas,
my heart I unlace,
letting my feelings spoke,
in art's sanctuary,
I find my breathing grace.

Embracing my personal space,
it's the cocoon where I metamorphose
into my finest self.

Consistency is the safe space I crave
in a world constantly moving at lightning speed.
I dare not blink, in darkness or light,
for fear of losing sight.

Grounded in values,
my roots firm in the ground,
embodying honesty, integrity,
beliefs profound,
I may grow leaves or roots,
expand with each day's sway,
but never shall I walk away
from this path I obey.

Tough on the outside,
beneath the surface concealed,
a heart as tender as a petal,
its depths revealed.

In my world,
my reality reigns supreme,
where I'm always right,
in my own dream.
Labeled "stubborn" by some,
I persist in my trust,
in those matters,
I don't adjust.

A rock of stability,
embracing the comfort
of grounded existence.

I relished the familiar path to school each day,
but as time's river flowed,
new routes came my way.
from school to college,
and then to work's first day,
stability, a comforting embrace,
is what I cherish, I must say,
while change, though inevitable,
sometimes causes my mind to sway.

It's not merely the allure of a beautiful bag
or the opulence of an expensive car,
nor is it just about possessing an item to flaunt.
It transcends surface value.
Those who observe can discern
the toil and determination invested
to attain it.

All my bank accounts in order,
"7 rings " by Ari on the radio,
a wishlist for the next shopping spree,
meticulously in tow,
in my life, nothing's luck or coincidence,
you should know.

As for spontaneity,
it's like mixing oil and vinegar,
a combination that,
in my world,
doesn't easily confer.

Sensuality blooms in their every move,
the touch, the taste, a sensory groove.
They savor life's pleasures with delight,
in love and art, their senses take flight.

They hold a profound reverence for the past,
recognizing that history provides a roadmap to cast,
guiding steps toward the future, steadfast,
in this wisdom, their understanding is vast.

Resilient and unwavering,
conquering challenges
with determination.

There's something comforting about watching paint dry,
or placing breadcrumbs and patiently waiting for birds
to come and pick them up,
or sitting in the hairdresser's chair
without moving while they cut your hair.
It feels like the earth slows down,
just for me.

In the realm of steadfast souls they reside,
Taurus, the guardian of stability and pride.
With earth beneath their feet and strength in their core,
they weather life's storms, forever secure.

Practicality as their armor,
finding solutions
in life's complexities.

Once set in their mind,
consider it locked in stone –
their unwavering conviction
leaves little room for change.

Fashion is my fluent tongue,
where each piece I choose
becomes a word in the story of my self-expression,
crafting a unique narrative of who I am.
Fashion isn't just what I wear,
it's how I communicate,
leaving an impression that lingers
long after I've walked away.

My actions will always speak,
that's the key,
more than words,
they unveil the real me.

In a world that rushes by with such haste,
will I ever find where my soul feels truly placed?

Taurus

I am reserved,
until I'm not,
you see,
not truly shy,
but quiet,
letting life before me,
observing first,
before I decide how to be.

Their nightmare scenario?
Drowning in chaos,
unpredictability's flow,
they prefer life with a dash of stability,
you know.

My anger can erupt swiftly,
uncontained,
holding it in would be self-betrayed.

Master of comfort,
I craft a sensual environment where the intertwining
embrace of coziness and comfort forms a sanctuary
so inviting, you'll never wish to depart.

Materialistic tendencies they may possess,
but comfort and luxury, they do address.
They appreciate the finer things in life,
surrounding themselves with beauty, they thrive.

LOVE AND
RELATIONSHIPS

Taurus in love

When a Taurus is in love, their devotion knows no bounds. They become a pillar of unwavering loyalty and steadfast affection. With their sensual nature, they shower their partner with love, embracing the pleasures of physical touch and intimate moments.

A Taurus in love is deeply committed and seeks stability and security in their relationship. They value the comfort of a stable partnership and will work tirelessly to create a solid foundation built on trust and mutual understanding.

Their love language often involves expressing their affection through acts of service, providing for their loved one's needs, and creating a nurturing environment. They find joy in pampering their partner with indulgent gestures and sensual experiences, ensuring that their love is felt in every touch and shared moment.

While Taurus can be possessive at times, it stems from a place of protecting what they cherish. They want to create a safe and loving space.

In love, a Taurus seeks a partner who appreciates their loyalty, sensuality, and commitment to building a solid foundation. They want a love that is both passionate and stable, where they can share their dreams, enjoy the finer things in life, and create lasting memories together.

Taurus in friendships

Friendship with a Taurus can be a rewarding experience. Taurus is known for being a loyal and dependable friend who will always be there when you need them. They have a calm and steady presence that can be comforting and reassuring in times of stress.

Taurus is also practical and down-to-earth, which means they can offer grounded and sensible advice when you need it. They tend to be good listeners and are often great at providing emotional support to their friends.

That being said, Taurus can also be stubborn and set in their ways. They may have a hard time compromising or changing their mind once they've made a decision.

Additionally, they can be quite materialistic and enjoy the finer things in life, which may make them less interested in doing low-budget activities with their friends.

Overall, a friendship with a Taurus can be a great one, as long as you're able to appreciate and navigate their unique traits and qualities.

I move with caution,
having felt the searing burn,
behind this rugged exterior,
a tender heart does yearn,
for the fear of another hurt,
it would painfully discern.

With a crush,
a Taurus' senses stir and soar,
every touch and word from their love,
they adore,
leaving indelible marks on their soul,
forevermore.

Comforting creamy pasta, cozy blankets,
silent cuddles, and a movie night –
that's the kind of love I yearn for,
a love as warm and soothing,
as a familiar melody on a chilly night.

In gentle grace, strength resides,
softness and strength by love's side.
Sensitive, yet with boundaries clear,
respect and love are always near.

Do not ponder my departure,
if you failed to relish the tranquility
that a well-crafted shared routine brings.

Amidst the checkered picnic blanket,
under roaming clouds so free,
surrounded by blooming flowers,
all I hear are your words, like birds,
setting my soul free.

If you perceive me as quiet and dull,
you've yet to truly encounter
the depth of my thoughts,
the fervor of my passions,
and the adventures
I harbor within.

I love like the coziness and tastiness
of a perfectly aesthetic picnic amidst flowers in the park.
Like the little child,
yearning for comforting hugs and hand-holding.
Like that teenager,
smiling at you from across the classroom
but quickly looking away when you catch my gaze.

In one special night with you,
my senses overflowed with delight. After a luxurious spa
experience, we ventured into the kitchen, creating culinary
magic together. Amidst the delightful mess, we shared a
meal that was not only delicious but also the most
wholesome and heartwarming experience. It felt like a
beautiful story in a movie just made for us.

In love, Taurus stands tall and strong,
with a heart that beats a steady song.
Passionate flames ignite their desires,
fanning the sparks of love's eternal fires.

Embracing a shared routine,
we find our rhythm and connection,
dancing to the same harmonious sound of life.

I toil tirelessly for my life's desires,
so don't be taken aback if I choose
not to share what's rightfully mine.
Remember,
jealousy can be a silent expression of love.

A sturdy foundation on fixed earth,
unwavering and true,
a lifelong soil, if tended,
it will always renew,
but if left to parch,
cracks may start to ensue,
regular care ensures our bond
remains steadfast and glue.

I was happy with the handpicked wildflowers,
and when you began calling me your wildflower.
I was happy with the Chinese takeout movie nights,
and how we cuddled even after the second movie ended.
I was happy with our daily walks,
and how you held my hand the entire time.
I was happy with us.

Sensuality flows
through their veins,
igniting passions.

Don't mistake my need for space
as a sign of detachment;
it's my way of nourishing my soul
and finding inner balance.

A Taurus' dating profile would read:

"Looking for someone who can keep up with my stubbornness, match my love for food, and appreciate my unwavering dedication to Netflix marathons. If you can handle my snuggly bull tendencies and understand that I'm only serious about tacos, then let's swipe right and enjoy a love as stable as my favorite armchair."

In the friend group,
only with my chosen few,
I am the anchor,
providing stability and reliability,
my loyalty shining true.

Sensual beings who find beauty
in the simplest pleasures,
their touch ignites a fire
that awakens the senses.

It's not my anger that should raise concern,
you see,
for when I'm angry,
it's a sign that you still matter to me.
worry not about my anger,
it's a sign that I still care,
but when silence lingers,
that's when we're in a state of disrepair.

Stability and comfort, in everyday's embrace,
romance in the little things, love's gentle grace.
Savoring cuisines, each bite a sweet surrender spun,
that's when I knew for sure, you were the one.

With eyes that see the beauty within,
devotion blooms, where love begins.
A promise kept, through thick and thin,
a bond unbreakable, hearts locked in.

The quest for stability led me
to build my home around someone,
only for them to leave,
and my roots found themselves
alone in that house.

Consistency,
the golden key that turns,
unlocking the door
to their heart's yearns.

A Taurus friend is like a fine wine –
they only get better with age.
Their loyalty and unwavering support
will only deepen as the years go by.

In a world without second chances,
trust is a rare commodity.
If you don't count yourself fortunate,
be prepared to see me depart.

A gentle massage,
soft sheets,
our favorite playlist for those evenings,
dessert awaiting on the nightstand,
candlelight flicker in the air,
Love,
an unspoken promise,
whispered softly there.

With you, I find grounding, like a child in a flower
meadow, running fingers through the grass without fear of
getting dirty. Lying beside you, our hands brush by chance
as you share your dreams, and time stretches on,
unhurried, hours passing in stillness.

When a Taurus falls in love,
their passion knows no bounds.
Their heart and soul consumed,
by the one that they've found.

Their touch is warm and tender,
their embrace, strong and true.
A Taurus love, a flame that burns,
with a heat that's ever new.

Their loyalty, unwavering,
their devotion, without end.
A Taurus love, a promise kept,
a bond that will never bend.

In a relationship, a Taurus
will shower their love with care.
Their partner, the center of their world,
their love, a constant and rare.

Their sensuality, a gift to share,
a Taurus touch, a heavenly bliss.
Their connection, deep and profound,
a love that cannot be dismissed.

So if you find yourself in the arms
of a Taurus loving embrace,
treasure the passion and warmth they bring,
and let their love light up your space.

The human embodiment
of the phrase 'ride or die.'
They'll stick by your side
through thick and thin,
no matter what.

Cooking for you,
rubbing your back while reading,
sending you outfit inspiration,
taking your hand while you drive,
lighting all the candles before you came home,
asking you about everything from your past,
observing all the details.
Did you hear my 'I love you'?

The abrupt shifts, the absent caress,
the 'I've dined at work' confess,
the dearth of compliments,
spontaneous nights with the friends to rest,
I sensed it drawing near,
this change's address.

Worry not about life's material comforts,
my dear,
the bathtub bubbles,
the wine,
the expensive food,
it's clear,
I relish the finer things,
crystal clear.
with dedication and hard work,
I steer,
towards a life of luxury,
together,
without fear.

Taurus

With loyalty as their guiding light,
they stand beside their love, day and night.
Through stormy seas or skies serene,
their love endures, forever keen.

In laughter and tears, they're always near,
to lend an ear or wipe a tear.
With a heart so warm and a spirit so kind,
in their friendship, solace you'll find.

In the dance of love,
seeking a partner
who moves in sync,
step by step,
creating a rhythm
of reliability and devotion.

Love's warmth radiates
from their embrace,
melting hearts.

Slow and steady,
a solid foundation,
unshaken by the storm.
In this house we've built,
we find our sanctuary.

Though the pain is deep,
Taurus' steady nature
helps them find stability
amidst the chaos of a breakup.

Can I trust again after heartbreak,
or will everything crumble
in half-hearted despair?

My quietness speaks volumes
about the depth of our connection.

In their arms, comfort and warmth reside,
a love that blossoms with each passing stride.
Through life's ups and downs, they remain,
a rock-solid love that nothing can tame.

My loyalty is unbreakable,
my patience is unmatched,
and my heart is filled
with unwavering devotion.

Taurus in love,
steadfast and true,
with a heart so loyal,
they'll always stay with you.

Taurus' biggest turn-off is someone
who tries to rush them in the bedroom.
They prefer to savor every delicious moment,
so take your time and let the passion build.

Taurus' biggest turn-on is someone who knows their way around the kitchen and can whip up a mouthwatering meal that sets their taste buds on fire.
Foodgasm guaranteed!

A perfect match is a soulmate
whose presence feels like coming home.

When a Taurus gives you their word,
you can take it to the bank.
They're as loyal as they come.

In a world of fleeting acquaintances,
Taurus prefers the intimacy of a small circle,
where true friendships can flourish
and withstand the test of time.

Sensual whispers dance upon their lips,
Taurus, the embodiment of passionate trips.
With every touch, they awaken desires,
setting hearts ablaze with their sensual fires.

When Taurus loves,
they take 'keeping an eye on you' to a whole new level.
Don't be surprised if they start secretly following you
with binoculars or installing hidden cameras.
Just remember, it's all in the name of love...
or maybe a touch of paranoia.

With a crush,
their normally composed self
starts tripping over their own words
like a clumsy puppy chasing its tail.

Embracing the solace of our wellness haven built at home,
we discover our own little sanctuary,
where troubles cease to roam.

Culinary adventure,
love goes through the stomach,
melodic laughter,
caring calls,
butterfly kisses,
"Count on me,"
hugs spoke
of belonging,
endless devotion,
bed of roses,
my forever

In the cosmic ballet,
Venus takes center stage,
captivating hearts
with its alluring grace.

Same time, same place,
our coffee shop's embrace,
traditions bind me,
no matter where I chase,
the people I need,
a warm feeling like home,
no need for big crowds,
together we roam.

Taurus' love language is like a slow dance in the kitchen. They'll sway to the rhythm of love while whipping up a gourmet meal, occasionally spilling ingredients and sharing a laugh. Who knew cooking together could be so romantic and messy?

Taurus' love language is like a warm, fluffy blanket
that swaddles you in their affection.
They'll spoil you with snuggles,
homemade cookies,
and endless Netflix marathons.
Get ready for a love that's as cozy
as a bear in hibernation!

I tread with caution,
wary of the fall,
for when I do,
you become my all.

Their ideal partner,
with patience strong and grace,
appreciates their love for comfort,
sets a steady pace.
To their insatiable hunger
for both food and affection,
they embrace,
like a saint with snacks and soothing rubs,
in this love's space.

My patience is unyielding,
but once you cross the tipping point,
there's no retreat.
I don't readily forgive
because to do so
would be a betrayal of myself.

Having demonstrated your worth in my world,
I offer you the richness of my resources,
a treasury of time, wealth, love, and tireless effort.

Love's patience knows no bounds,
as they wait for the right connection.

In the realm of relationships,
Venus guides us to seek harmony, balance,
and profound connection.

Like a doting gardener,
Taurus tends to their relationship
with sweet gestures and attentiveness,
but only when both partners
share the responsibility
of nurturing the connection.

In the inner circle's gentle glow,
my softer side shall show.

LIFESTYLE

The perfect day

Taurus' perfect day begins with the rising sun, casting a warm glow on the world around them. They wake up slowly, taking their time to stretch their limbs and savor the comfort of their cozy bed. A cup of steaming coffee or tea is the perfect way to start their day, sipping it slowly and savoring the rich flavor.

Next, they indulge in a hearty breakfast, whether it's a stack of pancakes with whipped cream or a savory omelette. With a full belly, they take on their day, whether it's heading off to work or enjoying a day of leisure.

Throughout the day, a Taurus takes their time with everything they do, they appreciate the small moments of pleasure in life, taking breaks to enjoy a delicious snack or a refreshing walk in nature.

As the sun begins to set, a Taurus enjoys a leisurely dinner with loved ones, relishing the flavors and the warmth of good company. After dinner, they might indulge in a relaxing bath or curl up with a good book, savoring the quiet moments of solitude.

Finally, as the day comes to a close, a Taurus settles into their soft bed, surrounded by plush pillows and blankets. With a contented sigh, they drift off to sleep, dreaming of all the joys that the next day will bring.

The perfect holiday

Taurus' perfect holiday is a captivating journey that combines the elements of comfort, indulgence, and sensory delight. They yearn for a vacation where they can unwind and fully immerse in the pleasures of life.

For the Taurus traveler, picture a serene beachside escape, where the warm sand embraces their bare feet, and the rhythmic waves serenade their senses. They bask in the sun's gentle caress, savoring the taste of tropical cocktails that transport them to a state of pure bliss.

Alternatively, a Taurus finds solace in a cozy cabin nestled amidst nature's embrace. Surrounded by majestic trees and pristine landscapes, they revel in the peaceful solitude and take delight in the simplicity of life. It's a place where they can reconnect with the earth.

For the Taurus seeking ultimate relaxation, a luxurious spa getaway beckons. They immerse themselves in tranquil environments, surrendering to the healing touch of skilled therapists. The soft melodies of soothing music and the aroma of essential oils envelop them, creating a sanctuary.

No matter the destination, Taurus' perfect holiday is a harmonious blend of comfort, luxury, and sensory pleasures. It is a time for them to escape the demands of daily life and recharge their spirits.

The perfect work environment

A perfect work environment for Taurus provides stability, structure, and a sense of security. They thrive in settings where they can work at their own steady pace and have a clear understanding of their roles and responsibilities.

In a Taurus ideal work environment, there is a strong foundation of stability and reliability. Taurus appreciates a predictable routine, where they can plan their tasks and projects accordingly. A Taurus feels most comfortable and productive in a structured and organized setting. They value a clear hierarchy and well-defined roles, allowing them to understand their place within the team.

Overall, a good work environment for Taurus combines stability, structure, security, autonomy, and aesthetics. When these elements align, Taurus can thrive, showcasing their dedication, attention to detail, and ability to produce high-quality work.

Additionally, a comfortable and aesthetically pleasing work environment enhances a Taurus productivity. They appreciate well-designed workspaces that prioritize both functionality and visual appeal.

The perfect vacation, a harmonious fusion,
relaxation, luxury, and indulgence in profusion.
A time to recharge, explore without intrusion,
savoring life's beauty in a serene conclusion.

A perfect vacation, a dream's embrace,
nature's serenity, delicious food, a tranquil space,
time to unwind, recharge, in this beautiful place,
a dream come true, life's gentle grace.

They thrive in workplaces with much light,
comfy chairs and nap pods, just right.

Taurus' perfect vacay is like a scene out of a movie –
think 'Eat, Pray, Love' meets 'The Great Gatsby'.

Their passion for craftsmanship
shines so bright,
be it woodworking, pottery,
or a creative flight.
in hands-on hobbies,
they find their delight,
bringing visions to life,
with all their might.

A perfect holiday is all about indulgence –
they won't be satisfied until they've eaten their weight
in delicious food and sampled every local wine.

In routines,
I discover solace and delight,
finding safety in the comfort
of knowing what each day may invite.

Bubble baths and face masks,
champagne in a glass,
ordering food in,
my safe space,
moments that last,
wellness Sundays,
my sanctuary,
unsurpassed.

In their work haven,
steadfast and profound,
a stable refuge,
like roots deep in the ground.

They find serenity in nature's gentle embrace,
gardening, hiking,
or simply nature's grace.
outdoors, their heart and soul interlace,
in its beauty,
they find their special place.

They understand 'me time'
like no other can,
a sacred self-care ritual,
part of their life's plan,
indulging in solitude,
their spirits expand.

For a perfect getaway,
Taurus seeks only the finest,
luxurious comfort,
where relaxation intertwines.
Delicious cuisine and drink,
a sumptuous feast,
time to unwind
and savor life's innermost dreams.

They value a work environment,
pleasing to the eye,
comfortable and well-designed,
where creativity can fly.
Spaces aesthetically pleasing,
where they're eager to apply,
their skills and passion,
beneath the open sky.

Taurus' perfect holiday is like a spa day on steroids –
they want to be pampered, relaxed, and rejuvenated,
all while sipping a glass of champagne.

A touch of luxury graces their residence,
creating an atmosphere
of indulgence and refinement.

Through art, we speak in colors.
Through music, our hearts find their rhythm.
Through fashion, we wear our souls on our sleeves.

For a perfect holiday,
it's all about crafting comforts –
a snug, inviting bed,
towels as fluffy as clouds,
a minibar stocked with delights.
These are the essentials of indulgence.

Their gaze,
a luminary of design's grace,
with a passion for fashion,
they find their place.
as stylists and trendsetters,
they leave a trace,
of style and elegance,
in life's embrace.

Flourishing at labor's call,
with steadiness and grace,
routine's familiar dance,
clear steps to trace,
cozy workspace's bounds,
roles meticulously outlined,
deadlines, at times, relent,
in this structured design,
content.

They seek solace
in life's simple grace,
cozy moments,
good food,
in a warm embrace.

When it comes to hobbies,
Taurus has a special talent
for collecting random objects.
Their home could double
as a museum of oddities.

LIFE LESSONS

Embrace flexibility, dear Taurus,
for sometimes the best opportunities come
when you're willing to step
outside your comfort zone.

Remember, life is not just about material possessions,
but also about the intangible joys
and connections that bring true fulfillment.

Embrace your sensual side,
for it adds richness and pleasure
to every experience.

Learn to trust in the process of change,
for growth often lies in embracing new experiences
and letting go of the familiar.

Open your mind to new perspectives
and be open to different ideas.

Open your heart to vulnerability,
for true strength lies not in stubbornness,
but in the ability to adapt and grow.

Challenge your possessiveness,
for true love and friendship
thrive in an environment
of trust and freedom.

Cherish your loyal and steadfast nature,
for it forms the foundation of lasting relationships.

Take risks and step outside
of your comfort zone
to unlock new possibilities.

Explore your adventurous side, dear Taurus, for life's greatest adventures often await beyond the confines of your comfort zone.

Note to self, Taurus:
Keep a stash of snacks nearby
to ward off the hangry monster within.
Your loved ones will thank you!

Cherish your appreciation for beauty,
as it helps you find joy
in the simple wonders of life.

Let go of your resistance to change,
for it is through change
that you discover new horizons
and unlock your full potential.

Practice self-reflection, dear Taurus,
and strive for personal growth,
as true wisdom comes from a willingness
to learn and evolve.

Hold onto your patience,
for it allows you to navigate challenges
with grace and composure.

ABOUT THE AUTHOR

As I embark on this literary journey, I, Denise Grace, welcome you into my world as a proud Libra and a passionate devotee of the mystical realm of astrology. Being a Libra myself, I have always felt a deep connection with the harmony-seeking nature of my zodiac sign. It is this intrinsic connection that ignited my curiosity and fascination with the celestial wonders that shape our lives.

From the moment I discovered the intricate art of astrology, it felt as though a veil had been lifted, revealing a universe of wisdom and insight. As a Libra, I found solace in the profound emphasis on balance, beauty, and meaningful connections that astrology offers.

Through the pages of this book series, I aim to share my love for astrology and its profound impact on our lives, all while keeping it light-hearted and playful. The intention is not to delve into the depths of complex astrological theories or make definitive predictions, but rather to celebrate the unique quirks and qualities of each zodiac sign.

Made in the USA
Las Vegas, NV
31 October 2023

79891300R00118